OWEN'S GUIDE TO SURVIVAL

MEREDITH RUSU

COPYRIGHT

Photo ©: background leaves throughout: Kanea/Shutterstock.

ISBN 978-1-338-23802-0

10 9 8 7 6 5 4 3 2 1 18 19 20 21 22

Printed in the U.S.A. 40

First printing 2018

Book design by Jessica Meltzer

TABLE OF CONTENTS

TABLE OF CONTENTS

WHILE V
MEET LE
OWEN

COME ON.
THIS WILL BE FUN!

INTRODUCTION

Hey there. Owen Grady here. Legendary dinosaur trainer and all-around good guy. Welcome to Jurassic World. You're going to like it here. We do pretty cool work. Training dinosaurs for rescue missions. Top-of-the-line equipment. We've spared no expense.

Since you're reading this book, I'll bet you're excited to head on into the park and meet some dinosaurs. Nice. Just remember, Jurassic World isn't a place for silliness. Dinosaurs are cool, but they're also dangerous. Hmmm . . . that sounds harsh. Pretty sure the park execs wouldn't want me telling visitors that. Let's try again. If a dinosaur is smiling at you, it's because it thinks you look delicious. Nope, still too strong. Okay, how about this: If you practice safety first, you'll have a good time.

And that's why I'm here! They don't call me a legendary dinosaur trainer for nothing. I've learned a thing or two about these bad boys. And I'm going to teach you everything you need to know in order to survive Jurassic Wor—hold on. Just got a text from Claire, the park operations manager (basically the boss). Can't say "survive." Whew, boy. This is going to be a looooong ride. Let's just say by the end of this book you'll be able to appreciate Jurassic World for all it has to offer. And maybe you'll even pick up a bit of dinosaur-training expertise, too!

WHAT IS JURASSIC WORLD?

Jurassic World is a place of fun and family where fossils come alive! It's located on an island in the middle of nowhere, and real-life dinosaurs live, play, and eat here just like they did back in the Jurassic era! You're probably wondering how that's possible. Dinosaurs went extinct millions of years ago, right? Well, it turns out scientists found bits of dinosaur DNA trapped inside mosquitos, which were trapped inside pieces of amber, and that amber was frozen inside ancient glaciers, and by using the advanced science of genetic engineering . . .

Wow. That got complicated real fast. Here's all you really need to know. Dinosaurs live in Jurassic World exactly like they did millions of years ago, and now we humans can walk right alongside them! What could go wrong?

WALKING WITH DINOSAURS IS COOL!

(WHEN FOLLOWING THE PROPER SAFETY PROTOCOL)

Well, there was that one time it went wrong a bunch of years ago, when the island was called Jurassic Park. The folks back then could have really used a safety video or maybe even a handy little guide like this one. A park employee didn't follow the rules, dinosaurs got loose and chased a bunch of people . . . it was a bad day. But now Jurassic World does have a safety video, along with lots of safety equipment and warning signs. So, it's totally safe!

STEEL GATES

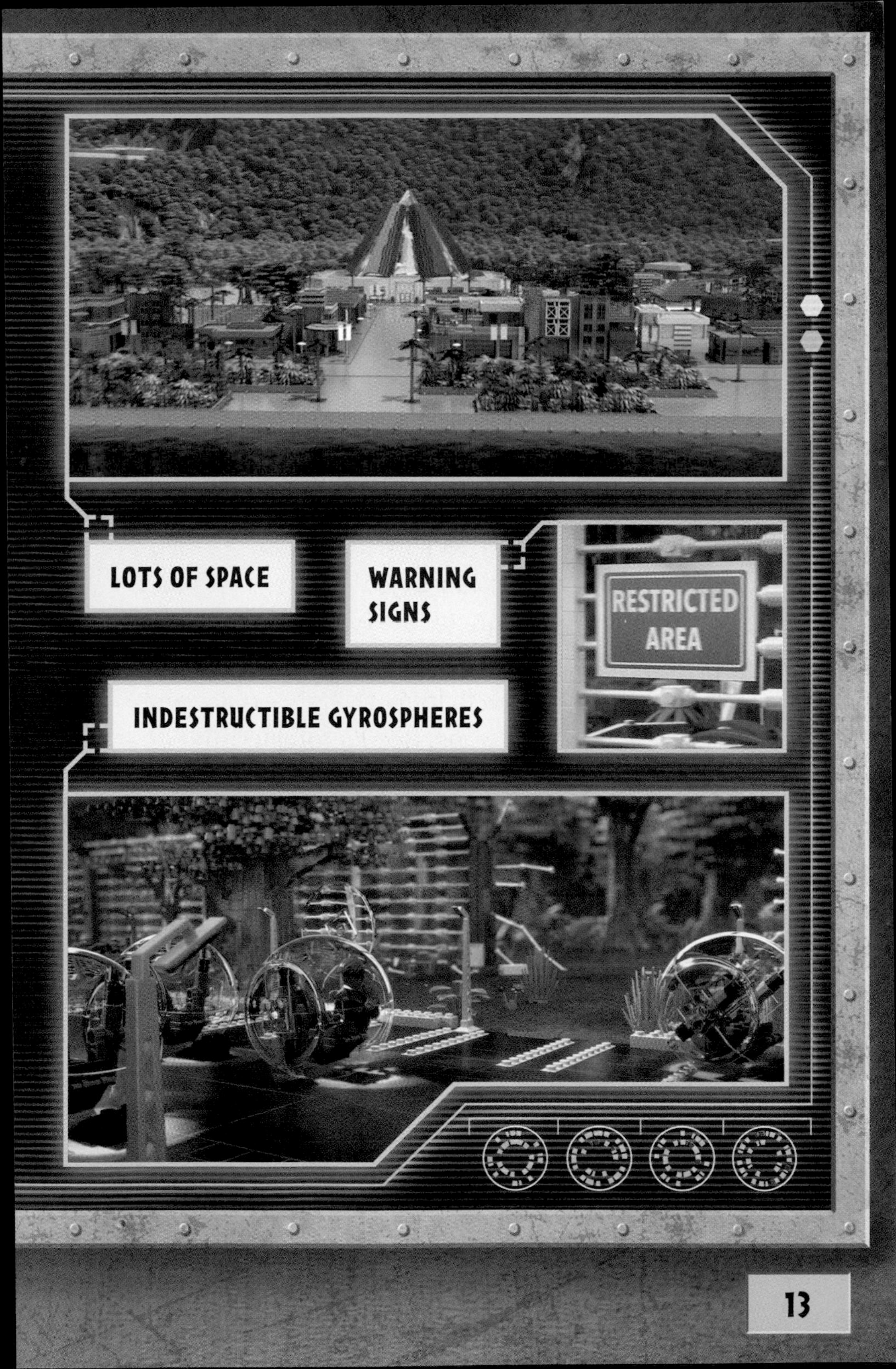
LOTS OF SPACE
WARNING SIGNS
RESTRICTED AREA
INDESTRUCTIBLE GYROSPHERES

WHO'S AT THE PARK!

Naturally, it takes a team of highly certified professionals to run Jurassic World. These folks help keep the park running and the dinosaur mayhem down to a bare minimum.

THIS IS CLAIRE.
She's the operations manager of Jurassic World and is always coming up with great ideas for new park attractions to keep visitors entertained. If you tell Claire she can't do something, there's a 99.9 percent chance she'll make it happen. That leftover 0.1 percent chance is for the times she's already made it happen.

SIMON MASRANI is the owner of the company that owns the company that owns Jurassic World. He loves cool dinosaurs almost as much as he loves flying helicopters and playing video games. (When he does both at the same time, he's gonna have a bad day.)

DR. WU is the lead scientist for Jurassic World. His technology combines the features of different dinosaurs together into mega hybrid dinosaurs.

VIC HOSKINS is the head of park security. It's the perfect job for him, because he loves tracking down and capturing escaped creatures. It's also the worst job for him, because he's not really a team player.

LET'S GET THIS DINOSAUR PARTY STARTED

So now that you know a little bit about the park, let's head on in through those fifty-foot-tall, double-thick steel gates and get down with some dinosaurs! Just remember to stick close, or there's a good chance you could end up a dinosaur's lunch. I'm kidding! Kind of.

OWEN'S GUIDE TO:
KNOWING YOUR DINOSAURS

KNOWING YOUR DINOSAURS

LESSON #1 ABOUT JURASSIC WORLD: Dinosaurs are dangerous creatures. They are NOT pets. But you can have a fun time hanging out with them if you know which dinosaurs are friendly and which aren't. For example, some dinosaurs are herbivores, which means they only eat plants. They're cool to take a selfie with. Other dinosaurs are carnivores, meaning they only eat meat. What does that mean? It means put the selfie stick down and move far, far away.

If a dinosaur is snarling and growling and spitting goop, there's a good chance it's not selfie material.

Here's a handy checklist to help you remember which dinosaurs are herbivores (friendly!) and carnivores (less friendly!).

DINOSAURS THAT WILL EAT LUNCH WITH YOU:

BRACHIOSAURUS: Eats leaves for lunch.

TRICERATOPS: Eats bushes for lunch.

STEGOSAURUS: Eats salad for lunch. (It's on a diet.)

MAN IN DINOSAUR COSTUME:
Not actually a dinosaur. But probably calling someone to see if they want to have lunch.

DINOSAURS THAT WILL EAT YOU FOR LUNCH

DILOPHOSAURUS: Spits gross goop at things that move and then eats them for lunch.

T. REX: Eats anything that moves for lunch.

VELOCIRAPTOR (YOU CAN JUST CALL THEM "RAPTORS"): These guys are scary, sure, but they're also my buddies. Training Raptors is my specialty, and they're very smart.

MEGAMEAN DINOSAURS

And then there are hybrid dinosaurs Dr. Wu creates in a lab. When Jurassic World needed a new attraction, Claire asked Dr. Wu to create the biggest, scariest dinosaur ever. You know, for kids. Using his cloning technology, Dr. Wu created the Indominus rex. It's part T. rex, part Raptor, has a little bit of chameleon DNA thrown in so it can change colors, and is all-around terrifying.

Also, it eats hot dogs. I mean, on top of anything else that moves inside the park.

But I guess the fact that it can turn plaid is kind of cool.

TRUSTY TIP #1:

REMEMBER:
DINOSAURS ARE
NOT PETS!

OWEN'S GUIDE TO: TRAINING DINOSAURS

DINOSAUR-TRAINING ESSENTIALS

Okay, on to the cool stuff. Dinosaur training! That's my job. Knowing how to train dinosaurs isn't necessary to enjoy Jurassic World, but it is a pretty handy skill to have. And who knows? Maybe you'd make a great dinosaur trainer! It takes years of practice, but really, training dinosaurs isn't so hard. It's mostly about patience, trust, and a little thing I like to call: showing them who's the *alpha* or the *boss* or the *big cheese* or the *fearless leader* or—well, you get the point.

ARE YOU READY TO LEARN SOME BASIC DINOSAUR-TRAINING MANEUVERS?
SIR, YES, SIR!

SHOWING THEM WHO'S THE ALPHA

I'm in charge of training the Raptors at Jurassic World. Why Raptors? Because they're pack animals. That means they work together in groups and take commands from one leader, called the alpha. As long as I make sure they always think of me as the alpha, we're good!

MY DINOSAUR TEAM

I work with four Raptors I've been training ever since they were babies. I know everything about them: their likes, dislikes, and which one sleeps with a stuffed Stegosaurus at night. They've even got cool code names: Blue, Charlie, Delta, and Echo.

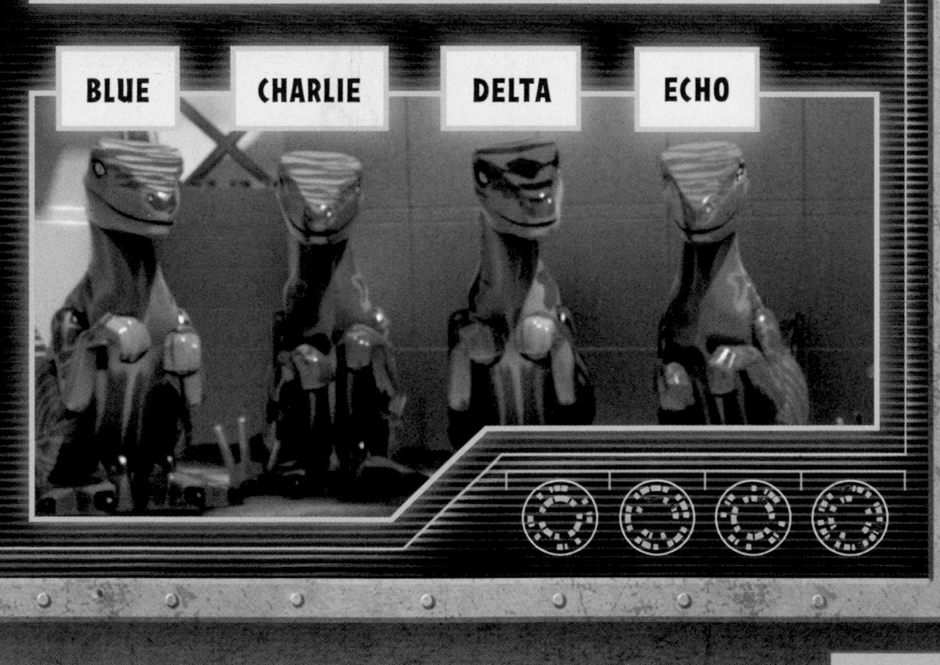

TRAINING TACTICS

Part of being the alpha is staying calm at all times and showing the dinosaurs that I'm in control. Like when I'm going through my morning routine in the Raptor pen. I'm in charge of when it's breakfast time, nap time, and playtime. Blue, Charlie, and me are having a staring contest right here. Am I sweating right now? Only I know for sure.

I SAW THAT, BLUE! YOU BLINKED!

And sometimes I have to use my training tactics on the fly. Like when I needed the help of Dr. Wu's wacky hybrid dinosaurs to help save the park from an Indominus rex rampage. They had never been trained before. But with my signature combination of steely stares and high-octane antiperspirant, I got them in line pretty quickly.

OKAY, YOU CRAZY HYBRIDS. TIME TO EARN YOUR KEEP!
TOTALLY NOT SWEATING.

DINOSAUR RIDING

Riding on dinosaurs is another big part of being a legendary trainer. At Jurassic World, we teach dinosaurs to go on rescue missions. By riding on them, we're able to make it to people who need help in the nick of time. Take me and my flying reptile buddy, for example (he's called a Pteranodon). Together, we can soar around the park helping employees stay out of sticky situations.

Like that time we caught Simon Masrani when he fell out of his helicopter. Boy, was he lucky we were on the job!

You've heard of a bird's-eye view. But have you ever heard of a Pteranodon's-eye view?

FANCY RUNNING INTO YOU UP HERE!

SPECIAL MANEUVERS

We also train dinosaurs in special maneuvers. Just the other day, I taught Dr. Wu's hybrid dinosaurs Special Maneuver Alpha 6. Sounds pretty impressive, right? It's really just a fancy way of saying "Go round up that renegade Indominus rex that's rampaging the Park!" But, hey, if you're going to be a legendary trainer, you need legendary special maneuver names, too.

WHAT WOULD YOU CALL YOUR DINOSAUR SPECIAL MANEUVER?

IT'S ALL ABOUT TRUST

The most important element of dinosaur training is trust. Remember how I told you dinosaurs aren't pets? They're not. So when it comes to training, I can never force a dinosaur to do something. (Actually, forcing them to do anything would pretty much guarantee a bad day.)

You and your dinosaur have to trust each other in order for the training to be a success. Even if you show them that you're the alpha, the only way to get a dinosaur to follow your commands is to earn their trust.

I taught my Pteranodon buddy how to do trust falls. That's where I'll jump from someplace high up, and my buddy will come to catch me. It wouldn't be possible if I didn't trust her and she didn't trust me. Also, trust falls look pretty cool.

TRUST FALLS

QUIZ: DO YOU HAVE WHAT IT TAKES TO BE A DINOSAUR TRAINER?

Okay, rookie. There's an opening and the position has YOUR name written all over it. Let's see if you've got the right stuff.

1) Do you like working with animals?

2) Are you calm, cool, and collected?

3) When assigned group projects, do you always take the lead?

4) Can you name ten different dinosaur species and the eras in which they lived?

5) Do your friends, family, and even random acquaintances refer to you as alpha?

6) Do you gravitate toward extreme sports, like jungle parkour and lion taming?

7) Do you own or can you borrow a super cool vest?

8) Do you have experience handling large reptiles that haven't walked the earth in several million years?

9) In case of an emergency, can you run SUPER fast or hide really well?

IF YOU ANSWERED YES TO 3 QUESTIONS OR LESS: Sorry to break it to you, rookie, but you have some pretty intensive training to do before you can go out into the wilds of Jurassic World and train some dinosaurs. But hard work pays off.

IF YOU ANSWERED YES TO 5 QUESTIONS: All right, you're on the right path. Training dinosaurs may be a little pie in the sky for you. But how about applying for a position at your local zoo? Good place to start learning the ropes!

IF YOU ANSWERED YES TO 7 QUESTIONS: Now we're talking! You like dinosaurs AND have the gumption to train them. Raptors are still a little out of your league. But Claire is always looking for people to staff the Dinosaur Petting Zoo.

IF YOU ANSWERED YES TO 9 QUESTIONS: Wow. You . . . you really answered yes to all nine questions? Huh. I'm impressed. Okay, rookie. You're in. See you outside the Raptor pen, 8:00 a.m. sharp. Don't be late. The Raptors like their breakfast on time, or else they get . . . cranky.

TRUSTY TIP #2:

NEVER TURN
YOUR BACK TO
THE CAGE.

OWEN'S GUIDE TO:
DRESSING THE DINOSAUR-WRANGLER WAY

OWEN'S OUTFIT ESSENTIALS

At Jurassic World, you can only do your job if you have the proper attire. Would you play a team sport without a uniform? No! Would you go into space without a space suit? Of course not. Would you sleep without pj's? Well, maybe, but the jungle is hot and my trailer doesn't have AC and—why am I telling you this? Anyway, what matters is if you're going to tango with dinosaurs, you need the right duds.

SCRUFFY APPEARANCE

So it doesn't look like you care too much. Dinosaurs like to work for attention.

COTTON SHIRT

Nothing breathes like cotton.

UTILITY VEST

Hidden compartments for snacks

DURABLE PANTS

If you thought grass stains were hard to get out, try getting out a dinosaur doo-doo stain.

KNIFE

This is really just for chopping veggies. A balanced diet is very important.

THE MANY LOOKS OF JURASSIC WORLD

Of course, not everyone at the park is a dinosaur trainer like me. In fact, I'm the only one I know! But that doesn't mean they don't need special gear for tackling their jobs, too.

SCIENTIST STYLE: Nothing says "intelligent" like a lab coat and gloves.

VIP EXECUTIVE: A white business suit always stands out as official. Even more so when you pair it with your sleek smartphone and sharp haircut.

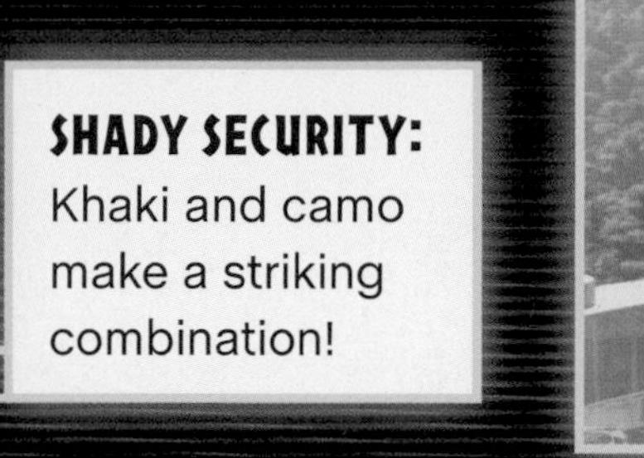

SHADY SECURITY: Khaki and camo make a striking combination!

LOOKS . . . LIKE A BAD IDEA

And while we're on the subject of dressing, let me address some outfits that will make it very hard to survive . . . uh, I mean, appreciate, Jurassic World. Lately, I've noticed these "bad idea" styles floating around that park. They really make you stop, scratch your head, and wonder, "Why would that look enter your brain?"

IT WAS CLAIRE'S IDEA, I SWEAR!

DINOSAUR COSTUME: I saw this weird dinosaur-costume dude running around the park the other day trying to avoid all the dinosaurs attracted to him. What did he think would happen if he dressed like a dinosaur? Whose idea was this?

I NEED A
NEW JOB.

HOT DOG COSTUME: Then, later, I saw the same guy walking around in a hot dog costume. He was even shoveling hot dogs into a crate to feed the Indominus rex while he was wearing the costume. Why would shoveling wieners require a costume? Who is he getting his fashion advice from?

HOMEMADE SAFETY GEAR: Then there's the case of this newbie who decided to don homemade safety gear while feeding the Dilophosaurus, the dinosaur that spits gross goop. I get it. We're stuck on an island and suitable clothing can be hard to come by. But trust me, handmade is not the way to go.

HERE, DINOSAUR,
DINOSAUR, DINOSAUR.
TIME FOR YOUR DINOSAUR
DIN-DIN.

DASHING OR DELICIOUS?

Quiz time! What Jurassic World style speaks to you the most? Choose one word from each column to complete your look. Then decide with your friends if your Jurassic World style will make you an alpha or make you lunch.

OLD	TAILORED	JEANS
GLOW-IN-THE-DARK	UTILITY	VEST
FLASHY	RIPPED	LAB COAT
WHITE	SMELLY	HOT DOG COSTUME
OFFICIAL JURASSIC WORLD	CAMO-PRINT	SOCKS

TRUSTY TIP #3:
RUNNING IS A LAST RESORT!

OWEN'S GUIDE TO:
COOL RIDES
AND GADGETS
WARNING: PHONES WILL CRACK UNDER PRESSURE.

RIDE ON

One of the questions I get a lot from visitors is "When will I get to walk with dinosaurs?" I know that we trainers get to ride on dinosaurs. But as a guest, the best way for you to appreciate Jurassic World is from inside the scientifically enhanced glass orb of a gyrosphere. These futuristic globes roll along the ground like a ball, but because of their gyrosphere technology, riders stay upright at all times. A gyrosphere's glass can sustain the impact of a flying projectile and protects against Dilophosaurus goop. Also, they look really cool.

GYROSPHERES

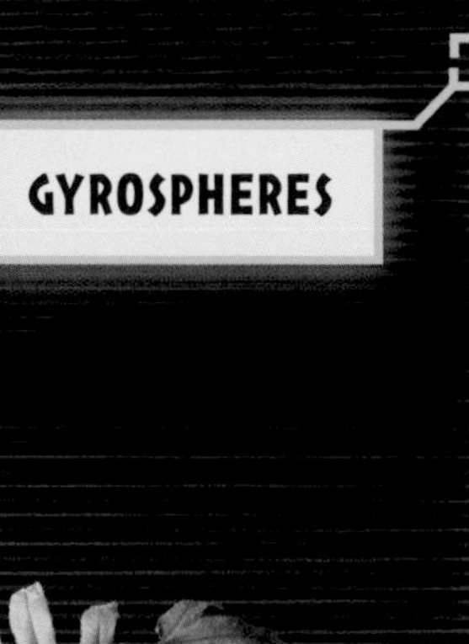

WHOA!!
Just make sure the parking brake is on, or you might be in for a wild ride.

NEVER RUN WHEN YOU CAN HIDE

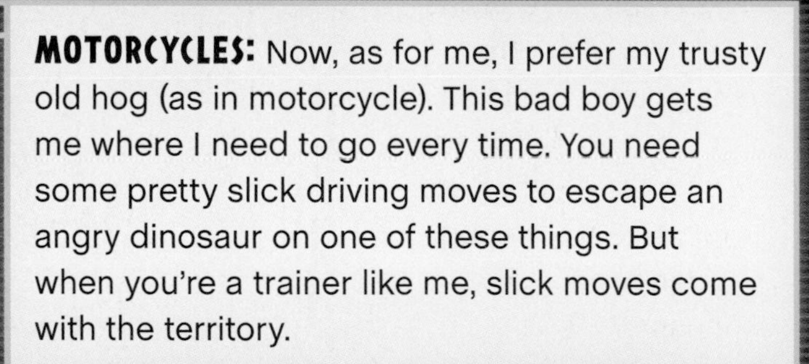

MOTORCYCLES: Now, as for me, I prefer my trusty old hog (as in motorcycle). This bad boy gets me where I need to go every time. You need some pretty slick driving moves to escape an angry dinosaur on one of these things. But when you're a trainer like me, slick moves come with the territory.

MOBILE RESEARCH MODULE: For the rest of the Jurassic World crew, research modules are their go-to modes of transportation. These vehicles have reinforced metal walls and forty feet of cable used to lasso dinosaurs. That comes in handy when you have to track down a renegade dinosaur. In the jungle. At night.

—Reinforced titanium walls
—Monster-truck tires
—Forty feet of tow cable

IT MAY BE PITCH-BLACK OUT HERE, BUT I FEEL SUPER SAFE!

—Steel roll cages
—Spare tire
—LED headlights

4X4: And when all else fails, jump into a trusty 4x4 to make a getaway. You're always better off riding inside a vehicle than running on foot from a dinosaur. I really can't emphasize this enough: You cannot outrun a dinosaur.

ARE YOU SURE YOU HAVE A LICENSE TO FLY THIS THING?
YOU WORRY TOO MUCH, CLAIRE. OF COURSE, I DO. KINDA . . .

HELICOPTERS: Of course, if you're looking for the airborne Jurassic World experience, then a helicopter is the only way to go. Just make sure your pilot has his license, otherwise you might crash into the Aviary, release all the flying Pteranodons, and have a really bad day. True story.

WHOOOOOAAAAA!
He absolutely does *not* have his license.

DINOSAUR-WRANGLING GADGETS

Sometimes in Jurassic World, accidents happen. Dinosaurs escape. Bad things follow. The best thing to do in these situations is seek shelter and leave first response to the professionals. We're highly trained in the art of dinosaur wrangling and have a trusty assortment of gadgets at our command.

THWACK!

NETS: Not just for hair anymore.

LASSOS AND SLEEPY-TIME DARTS: For when you need to round up a whole herd of escaped dinosaurs. (That really shouldn't be happening, but it does more often than you'd think. We should probably look into that.)

THE TICKLER: For when you need a dinosaur to spit something out. Like a large tree branch. Or a coworker.

TRUSTY TIP #4:

IF YOU'RE GOING TO FLY, MAKE SURE YOU TRUST YOUR PILOT!

OWEN'S GUIDE TO: DOS AND DON'TS OF JURASSIC WORLD

JURASSIC WORLD DOS AND DON'TS

So that about covers the basics for how we workers at Jurassic World keep things A-OK. But I'll bet you're thinking, "Owen, I don't want to work at Jurassic World. I just want to hang out with cool dinosaurs!" Well, everything I've just taught you still applies. But as a normal visitor to Jurassic World, you'll need to keep a few extra things in mind in order to make the best of it. And that starts with some simple dos and don'ts.

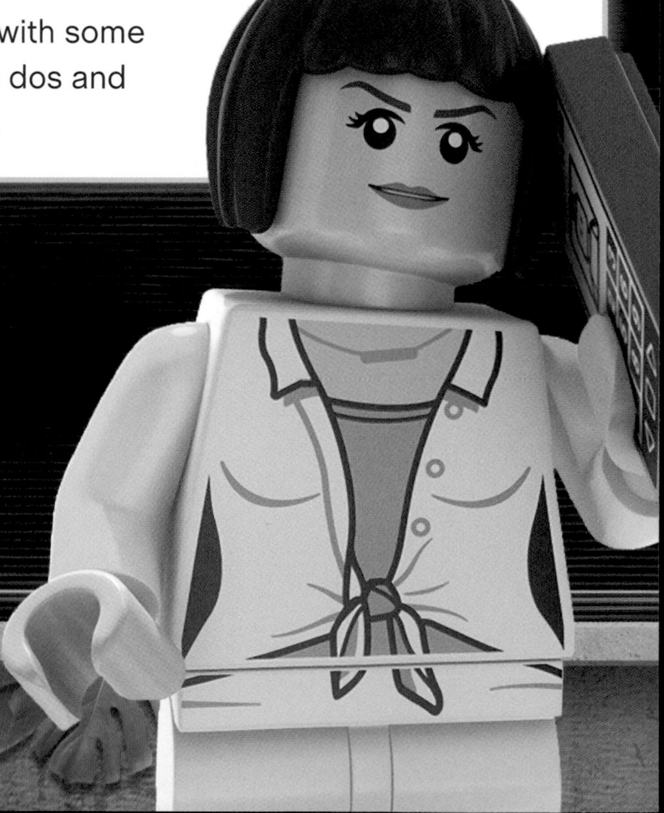

JURASSIC WORLD

Employee Safety Video

DO: WATCH THE SAFETY VIDEO

Claire hired a film crew to produce a special safety video for all Jurassic World employees that visitors might find helpful. As it turns out, it's not half-bad! Take a look.

JURASSIC WORLD PRESENTS: SAFETY AT THE PARK. PLEASE USE COMMON SENSE AT ALL TIMES, OR YOU JUST MIGHT FIND YOURSELF ON THE WRONG END OF AN OOPSIE.

LIKE THIS . . .

He tried to race a dinosaur. Now he's having a bad day.

OR THIS . . .

He wasn't paying attention to his surroundings. Bad idea.

OR THIS . . .

He teased a T. rex. Can you see the flaw in his logic?

OR ESPECIALLY THIS . . .

Carrying around loose hot dogs near the enclosures? One of Jurassic World's major no-nos.

WOW. I GUESS YOU NEVER CAN UNDERRATE THE VALUE OF GOOD OLD COMMON SENSE.

HMMM. FOR A PARK NOT SPARING ANY EXPENSE, YOU'D THINK THEY'D INVEST IN SOME STURDIER RAILINGS.

DO: WATCH OUT FOR FAULTY PARK EQUIPMENT

You don't want to discover after the fact that the railing you were leaning against overlooking the Raptor pen was not securely in place.

You also don't want to find out that the gate to the T. rex enclosure is malfunctioning. "Has that ever happened?" you might ask. Ha-ha . . . heh . . . okay. Yes. But it wasn't my fault.

I DON'T LIKE THE WAY SHE'S LOOKING AT ME . . .
I'M SURE THE GATE IS SECURE . . . THIS TIME.

SHOULD YOU GO HERE?

DO: READ THE SAFETY SIGNS

Seriously, so many catastrophes could be avoided if people just read the signs. Follow these clearly posted instructions, and you'll have a good day. Ignore them and it's bad-news Brachiosaurus.

SHOULD YOU OPEN THAT GATE?
UH, NO!
RESTRICTED AREA

DON'T: TRY TO CAPTURE THE DINOSAURS

Unless you're on a mission with all of park security to track down an escaped dinosaur, never ever go off on your own to capture a dinosaur. Don't be that guy. That guy always ends up having a bad day.

I'M THE HEAD OF PARK SECURITY, NOT A SOCCER BALL! YOU CAN'T PUSH ME AROUND LIKE THIS!

DOS AND DON'TS QUIZ:

Pop quiz! Didn't think there'd be any of those in this book, huh? Well, there is! You just read a bunch of common-sense dos and don'ts about Jurassic World. Let's see if you were paying attention. Answer the following questions with yes or no.

1) You see a hot dog lying on the ground outside the Raptor cage. Ooh! It looks clean. Should you eat it?

2) You see footprints leaving the Indominus rex's compound. Huh, she must have left. You probably have time for a quick look around her nest, right?

3) You stumble into Dr. Wu's lab. No one is around. All his technology looks so cool. Should you press a few buttons and see what happens?

4) Ooh! There's a hot dog costume in the lost and found at Jurassic World. What better way to make a few bucks than to sell hot dogs dressed as a hot dog? Why not put it on and sell these snacks outside the Indominus rex's compound?

5) All the gyrospheres have been ordered back to base due to a "containment anomaly." But you're sure it's nothing serious. It's time for some off-roading, right?

6) That cute hybrid dinosaur just purred at you. At least it sounded like a purr. Could have been a snarl. You're not sure. But it was adorable. Want to pet it?

Answers #1–5: No!
Answer #6: No. If you answered yes, congratulations. You just became dinosaur lunch.

TRUSTY TIP #5:

NEVER PLAY
HIDE-AND-SEEK
WITH A DINOSAUR.

OWEN'S GUIDE TO:
THINKING FAST

WALK LIKE A DINOSAUR

Hand in hand with common sense is thinking fast. In a place like Jurassic World, there isn't time to stop and smell the roses. When something goes wrong, it goes wrong at lightning speed. So if, despite your best efforts, you still find yourself on the wrong end of a dinosaur oopsie (it happens), the best thing to do is stay calm and use a dinosaur's abilities to your advantage.

TAIL SLIDING

Like . . . when Claire accidently crashed her 4x4 chasing the Indominus rex . . . and ended up on the Indominus's back! I shouted to her that the only way down was the old-fashioned playground way. Tail sliding!

YOU'D BETTER BE RIGHT ABOUT THIS, OWEN!

DINOSAUR HOPPING

Or like . . . when I needed to reach Simon before he fell out of the sky and became a Jurassic World pancake. My best bet was to play hopscotch along the backs of the Pteranodons.

THINK LIKE A DINOSAUR

Thinking like a dinosaur is another way to get out of sticky situations. Dinosaurs are intelligent creatures with both strengths and weaknesses. Sometimes, you can use those to your advantage. One of my Raptors' strengths is that they're pack animals. When the Indominus rex was on the loose, I knew I could trust my team to round her up.

It was a good plan at first. But little did we know that the Indominus was part Raptor, and could communicate with my team! She convinced them to help her take over the park! We had to think of a new plan, and fast!

ALL RIGHT, BLUE, CHARLIE, DELTA, AND ECHO. GET 'EM!

UH, OWEN, I AM NOT SURE THEY'RE LISTENING TO YOU.

That's when Claire realized we could use the Indominus's one weakness to our advantage instead. The Indominus rex loves hot dogs. So, bad news for the hot dog mascot guy. But good news for Park security, since they knew how to lure her back to her paddock!

YOU'VE JUST BEEN HOT-DOGGED!

KNOW YOUR WARNINGS

Here at Jurassic World, we use cautionary announcements to help Park guests know important information. Now, don't tell Claire I told you this—seriously, I could get in trouble—but the loudspeaker announcements are worded to keep everyone calm and not cause panic. The best way to appreciate Jurassic World is to know what each announcement actually means.

PARK CAUTIONARY ANNOUNCEMENTS

WHAT IT SAYS	WHAT IT MEANS
Valued patrons: Due to an unexpected shortage on hot dogs, all guests are encouraged to purchase alternate food choices.	The Indominus rex has eaten all the hot dogs . . . and is still hungry.
Attention, guests: Due to technical difficulties, the Aviary is now closed.	The Aviary has been smashed and wild Pteranodons are now on the loose.
Dear visitors: Unanticipated but standard power surges may cause lights to flicker. Do not be alarmed.	A dinosaur has chewed through the main power grid and the park now has no power.
Please be advised: Due to a containment anomaly, all guests must seek shelter immediately.	THERE'S A MEGAMEAN DINOSAUR ON THE LOOSE!

THINK FAST!

Ha! Surprised you with another pop quiz. You'll have to think faster than that to ace this one. Answer the questions below to see if your fast-thinking skills are up to speed or if they're as slow as a Raptor with a cold. (Ha! I crack myself up.)

1) When you get caught in an unexpected rainstorm, can you usually whip up an impromptu umbrella?

2) At the movies, do you note all the exits, keeping in mind that the nearest exit may be behind you?

3) When you're playing a team sport, are you able to use your opponent's weaknesses to your team's advantage?

4) If your normal route home from school is blocked, do you know every backup route and at least one shortcut?

5) Do you carry a flashlight with you at all times in the event of a power outage?

6) At a theme park, do you pay close attention to loudspeaker announcements?

7) If you were being chased by a dinosaur, would you run?*

QUIZ RESULTS: If you answered yes to every question except #7, congratulations! Your quick-thinking skills are top-notch.

*Ha! Trick question. Always ride away on a motorcycle. Never run.

TRUSTY TIP #6:
DON'T MESS WITH DINOSAUR DNA!

DNA
THE BUILDING
BRICKS OF LIF

SSIC WORLD,
MEET LEG
RY DINOSAUR TRAINER
OWEN
RADY!
WHILE VIS
ITING JURA

OWEN'S GUIDE TO: HANDLING CATASTROPHES

WHEN GOOD IDEAS GO BAD

All right, rookie. You're doing great. Let's keep up the pace. We've covered dos and don'ts, common sense, and thinking fast. What does that leave? Ah, yes. Good old-fashioned catastrophes.

No matter how much you prepare at Jurassic World, accidents happen. Like that time I started telling you about when the Indominus rex escaped from her paddock and wanted to snack on the hot dog guy. That was a classic catastrophe right there.

A GOOD IDEA . . .
Claire and Dr. Wu thought using hot dogs to train the Indominus rex to do tricks for park visitors was a great idea. I wasn't so sure.

WAIT, YOU FEED HER HOT DOGS?

I DON'T SEE A PROBLEM WITH GIVING HER HOT DOGS IF SHE LIKES THEM.

. . . GONE VERY BAD

Annnnnnnd, I was right. It was a very bad idea. Feeding the Indominus rex all those hot dogs spoiled her. She wanted even more! That's when she saw the guy in the hot dog costume. I think you see where this is going.

CORNERING THE MARKET ON HOT DOGS

We had to trick the Indominus back into her paddock. And that meant using her love of hot dogs against her.

Claire laid out every hot dog on the island leading right back to the Indominus rex's enclosure. We waited . . . and the Indominus took the bait! She started chowing down on hot dogs like a kid in a candy store. Would Claire's plan work?

IT'S FOOLPROOF.
I'VE LAID OUT EVERY
HOT DOG ON THE ISLAND.
SHE'LL HAVE TO COME
THIS WAY.

TEAMWORK

But there was one thing we never accounted for. The Indominus rex got a tummy ache from eating all those hot dogs, and she began attacking everything in sight! Now we really were in catastrophe mode!

We needed to pull together and work as a team to get her back under control. Handling catastrophes is next to impossible alone. But as a team, we had a shot.

We gave her all the sleepy-time darts we had, and even that wasn't enough to rein her in!

Meanwhile, my Raptors were still convinced they should help the Indominus rex take over the park. (I can't believe they let the Indominus trick them like that!) That's when Claire stepped up to the plate and showed the Raptors who was boss.

AS DINOSAURS OF JURASSIC WORLD, YOU ARE LEGALLY CONSIDERED EMPLOYEES. I ORDER YOU TO STOP AND HELP US, OR I WILL TAKE AWAY YOUR VACATION DAYS.

DINOSAUR POWER

The Raptors were back on our side, but the Indominus was still on the rampage. We were running out of ideas, and running out of time. It was up to me. I knew teamwork was the only thing that could get us out of this. And we needed to add some new players to our team . . .

. . . dinosaur players!

ALL RIGHT, YOU DYNAMITE DINOSAURS. TIME FOR A CRASH COURSE IN TRAINING. LET'S GO CORNER THAT INDOMINUS!

I trained the hybrid dinosaurs on the way over. (Impressive, I know. But it's kind of what I do). And they followed my instructions to herd the Indominus back into her paddock. The park was saved in the nick of time!

WHEN WAS A TIME YOU TOOK CHARGE AND SAVED A SITUATION FROM CATASTROPHE?

TRUSTY TIP #7:

HOT DOGS ARE FOR HUMANS. NOT FOR DINOSAURS.

OWEN'S GUIDE TO: WORKING TOGETHER

MAKE ANY TIME TEAMWORK TIME

So there you have it. Jurassic World's greatest idea turned into its biggest catastrophe, but then transformed once again into its biggest success story. All through the power of teamwork.

And that's really the most important lesson I can teach you if you're gonna—I'm just going to come out and say it—survive Jurassic World. You need to work together with your friends, and maybe even a few dinosaurs, in order to save the day. As I always like to say, there is no "i" in team. But there is an "i" in "dinosaur lunch."

Facing off against dinosaurs four-on-one: **BAD IDEA.**

Facing off against dinosaurs with your entire backup team: **BETTER IDEA**!

TRUST YOUR TEAM

And to work together, you have to trust your team. If you only believe in yourself, how can you expect your team to have your back? You have to show them that you believe in them, too, in order for teamwork to be a success.

Claire wasn't 100 percent sure she trusted me at first.

CLAIRE! JUMP!

WHAT?!?

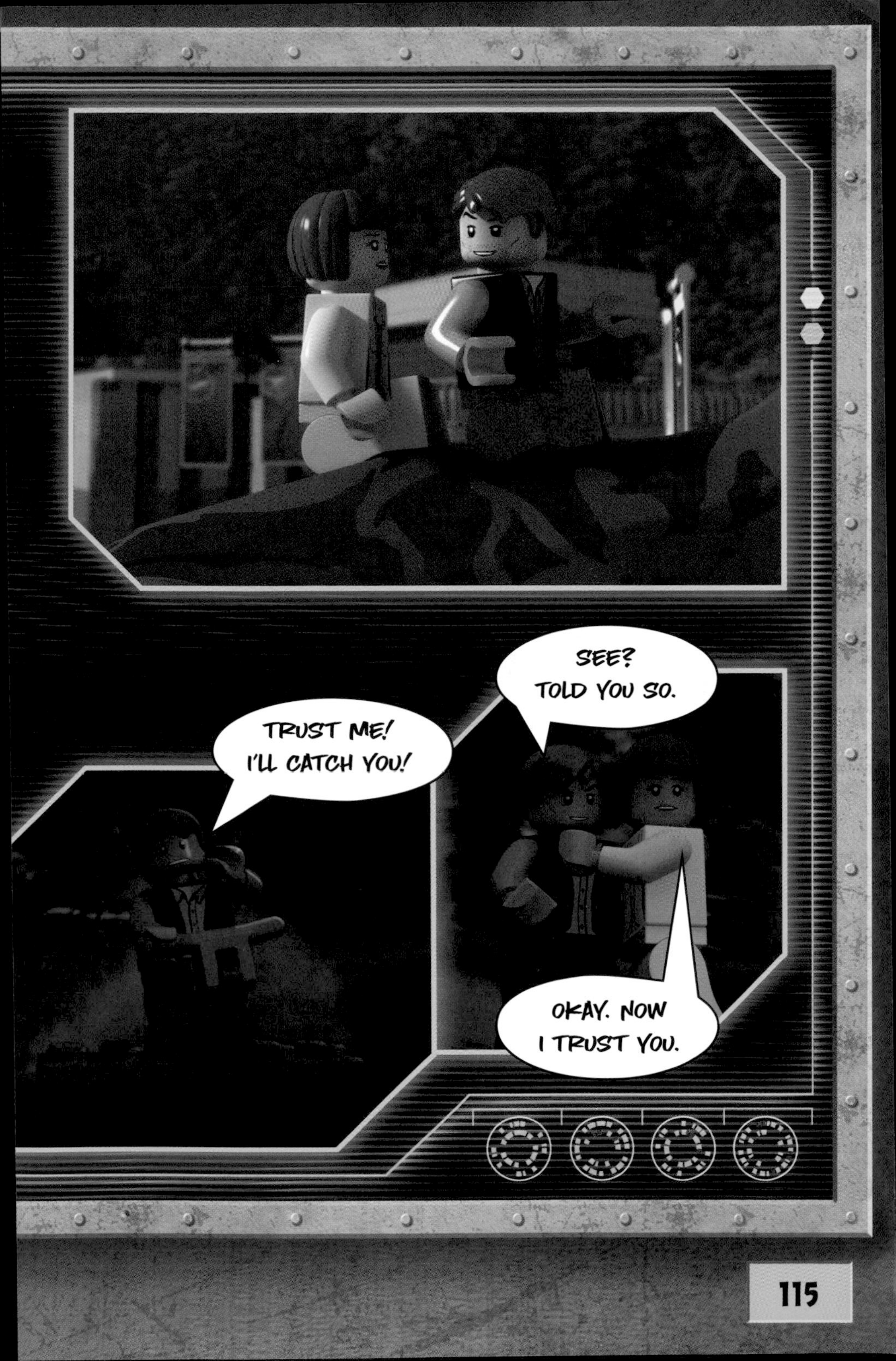
TRUST ME!
I'LL CATCH YOU!
SEE?
TOLD YOU SO.
OKAY. NOW
I TRUST YOU.

EARN THEIR TRUST IN RETURN

And for as much as you trust your team, you have to show them that you're trustworthy, too. How else do you think I'm able to get my Raptors to work together with me on rescue missions? It's all possible through trust.

TEAMWORK AND TRUST: ALWAYS A WINNING COMBINATION!

TRUSTY TIP #8:

TRUST ME.
I'M A
PROFESSIONAL.

GOOD-BYE

HOPE YOU ENJOYED THE PARK!

We made it! That went pretty well, I've got to say. Made it through the whole guide without any rookie catastrophes. Well done. I hope you had a good time at Jurassic World, learning about dinosaurs, common sense, and a few tricks of the trade. But the fun doesn't have to stop here. You can bring all the magic that is Jurassic World home with you in lots of neat ways. Turn the page for some colossally fun ideas!

CONTINUING THE JURASSIC WORLD FUN

1) BUILD YOUR OWN DINOSAUR: Unlike tinkering with DNA, it's totally safe (and even encouraged!) to build your own dinosaur completely out of LEGO bricks!

2) DESIGN A DINOSAUR COSTUME: Hey, if that guy can dress like a dinosaur at the park and make it out okay, you can make your own dinosaur costume at home and have a fantastic time for sure!

3) COOK UP YOUR OWN DINOSAUR RECIPE: Green Stegosaurus-shaped pancakes? T. rex–sized cereal balls? Hot dog casserole? Feed your inner beast! Make them out of LEGO bricks!

4) DRAW YOUR FAVORITE DINOSAUR: Or color a picture of an entirely new one. There are no limits to your imagination!

5) PRETEND THE PREHISTORIC WAY: Imagine your local park or your backyard is a prehistoric playground and walk like a dinosaur! Just make sure you trust your team before you set off into the wild.

6) MAKE PAPIER-MÂCHÉ DINOSAUR EGGS: Then put them on display in your room! They're a lot safer than the real ones—trust me.

7) PLAY A TEAM SPORT: And name your teams after your favorite dinosaurs!

8) WRITE A DINOSAUR STORY: Who knows? Maybe it will get made into a movie one day.

9) GO ON A JURASSIC WORLD-SIZED FAMILY ADVENTURE: To a theme park, a zoo, or even to see a movie. Because really, your family is the best team in the whole world.

LEGO®

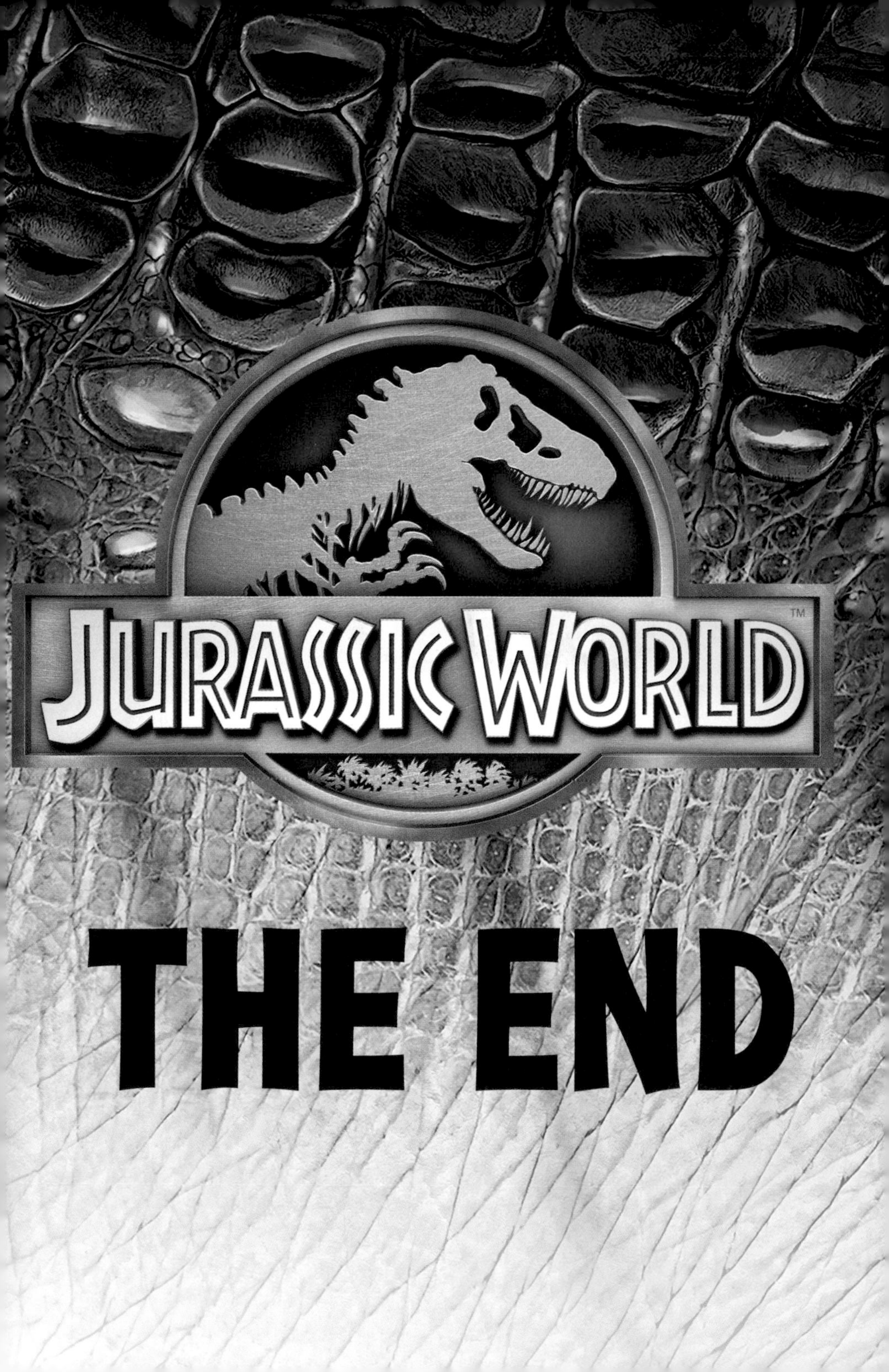
JURASSIC WORLD™
THE END

DON'T MISS!
LEVEL 2
LEGO
JURASSIC WORLD
BONUS! STICKERS INSIDE!
DINOSAUR DISASTER!
SCHOLASTIC
AVAILABLE NOW!